FOREWORD:

Hello reader, thank you for purchasing this eBook! My name is Luke and I am a colour blind school pupil who wrote this book to help others with the condition. I was inspired to write this book by things that my colour blindness has affected. All I wanted to do was create a short and informative guide that is easy to read and has all the right information. I hope that you enjoy this book and find it useful.

CONTENTS:

- Chapter 1 – *What is colour blindness and general facts*
- Chapter 2 – *Everyday problems faced by colour blind people*
- Chapter 3 – *Colour blindness and education*
- Chapter 4 – *Colour blindness and careers*
- Chapter 5 – *Advice on living with colour blindness*
- Chapter 6 – *My experience with colour blind glasses*
- Glossary

CHAPTER 1: WHAT IS COLOUR BLINDNESS AND GENERAL FACTS

There are many definitions for colour blindness; both scientific and non-scientific. Sometimes the condition is not necessarily known as colour *blindness* but rather as colour *deficiency*. However, the general description adopted for the condition is *"an inability to distinguish the differences between certain colours."* Colour blindness also manifests itself as an inability to distinguish between different *shades* of the same colour.

Though it is labelled as colour blindness; only a very small percentage of colour blind people actually see life as grey-scale. Most colour blind people can see colour, they just confuse certain colours and therefore may see two different colours or shades next to each other as one whole shade that is the same.

The condition was first discovered in 1794 by scientist John Dalton. He self-diagnosed; realising that he confused scarlet with green and pink with blue. Since then, research has uncovered the cause for the condition. It is known that most people are born with the condition and will stay with it for life. Some may contract the condition in old age or along with another illness or condition, but this may be a more complicated issue which will be explained later on in the chapter.

The recessive condition is usually *congenital* and is mostly passed from mother to son, with a daughter being a carrier of the gene. Most colour blind boys will have a colour blind grandfather on their mother's side, as their mother is a carrier. If their father has the condition but their mother is not a carrier, they are unlikely to inherit it. If a boy is colour blind, his sister is likely to be a carrier; meaning that her son would be colour blind. Though this is most commonly the case, girls can sometimes be born colour blind and mothers that are colour blind themselves will pass the gene on to their sons.

The easiest way to explain this is to talk about *chromosomes*. Boys have an *X* and a *Y* chromosome; whereas girls have two *X* chromosomes. The colour blindness gene fault is usually found on the *X* chromosome.

Girls inherit *two* X chromosomes, meaning that, even though their mother carries the faulty gene, they will not be born with the condition because their father has a *normal* X chromosome that is *dominant* (this "overpowers" the recessive trait on their mother's chromosome). This is why girls usually *carry* – they have the recessive gene from their mother but the normal gene from their father. If their mother is unaffected but their *father* is colour blind, they will *carry* the gene; as they will inherit a *dominant* gene from their mother; their brothers would most likely be unaffected. This is what happened to my mother, her mother is unaffected but her father is colour blind. Therefore, she is a *carrier* of the gene. Her brother is unaffected.

Girls will be colour blind when both their mother *and* father have a faulty gene. If their father is colour blind, his X chromosome will have the faulty gene which they will inherit. If their mother is also colour blind or is a carrier, their other X chromosome will *also* carry the faulty gene. This means that they will inherit both faulty genes – there will be no dominant normal gene to "overpower" the faulty gene. This is rarer, and is why far fewer girls are colour blind.

Boys, however, *must* inherit the Y chromosome from their father. This means that the only X chromosome they inherit will be the one that carries the faulty gene from their mother. This means that there is no other *dominant* gene from another X chromosome to "overpower" the recessive faulty gene.

To make this even simpler, two *dominant* genes will result in no change, a dominant *and* recessive gene will result in no change but the person being a carrier and two *recessive* genes will result in the condition being present and carried.

If you are still struggling to make sense of this, check the glossary at the back of the book. This contains definitions for some of the scientific terms.

Here are some diagrams to make it easier to understand:

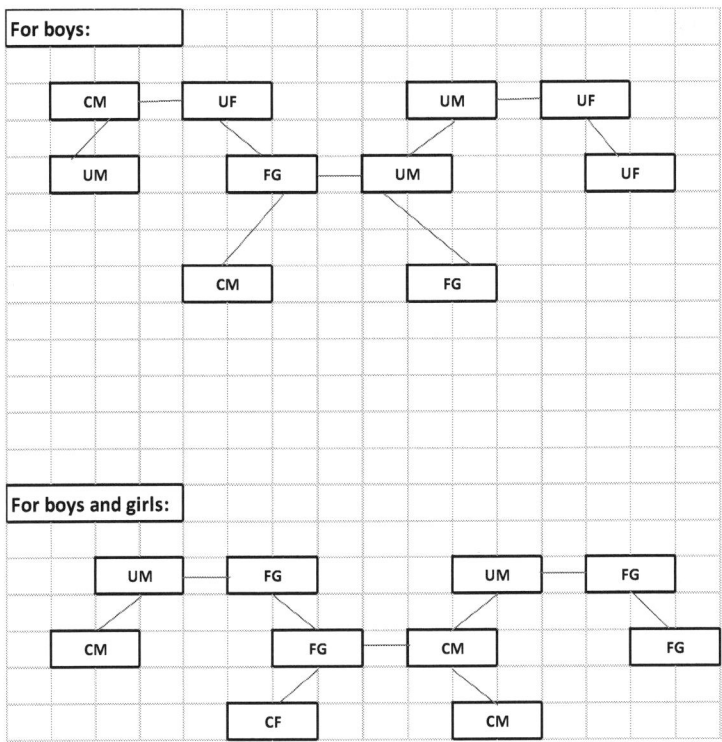

Key: letters	Key: person
UF	Unaffected female
UM	Unaffected male
FG	Female gene carrier
CM	Colour blind male
CF	Colour blind female

The scientific explanation for colour blindness is that there are issues with rods and cones, which are cells in the retina that effectively help us see colours and light intensity. Rods detect light intensity and are sensitive to low light levels. This partly explains why we see things as greyscale when it is very dark.

It is the cones, however, that make the largest impact with colour blindness. The cones are used by the brain to determine colour, and so are vital for seeing it. The cones are concentrated near the centre of vision and so play a vital role in sight. There are three types of cones: red, green and blue. Each of these detect wavelengths from their respective colour's parts of the spectrum.

There are many variations of colour blindness but each one is caused by an anomaly in the cones. The condition is caused when one or more of the cones are absent, do not work properly or detect a different colour from usual. Though it is usually a constant inability to distinguish between colours, some colour blind people can do this; but it takes them a few seconds to be able to. This can also happen to people with mild colour blindness (anomalies) – it takes them time to distinguish between less obvious colour differences which unaffected people would usually be able to see.

People with mild colour blindness usually have all three of their cones present. This is known as *trichromacy* and is present in non-colour blind people. Colour blind people who are trichromatic are known as *anomalous trichromats,* this means that one of their cones is faulty or out of alignment. About half of all colour blind people are thought to have anomalous trichromacy.

Dichromacy is usually present in those with moderate or severe colour blindness. Dichromacy means that one of the cones is either not present or completely dysfunctional. This effectively means that a whole segment of the colour spectrum cannot be interpreted in any way by someone with dichromacy.

Monochromacy means that two cones are either not present or completely dysfunctional. The condition is incredibly rare – only 1 in approximately 33,000 people have the condition. Monochromacy usually results in grey-scale vision where almost all perception of colour is lost.

Types of colour blindness split out even further and can sometimes be confusing to list and understand. The three types will end in either *–opia* or *–anomaly*. The former means that one of the three cones is absent or completely dysfunctional, so people with this condition will be *dichromatic* or *monochromatic*. The latter means that all three cones are present, but one is faulty. Therefore people with this condition are *trichromatic anomalous*.

These two categories split further into *Protanomaly/Protanopia, Deuteranomaly/Deuteranopia* and *Tritanomaly/Tritanopia.*

To put the following information simply, people with -opia cannot see the affected colour at all and people with -anomaly will have faulty perception of the affected colour; they may confuse different shades.

Protanomaly means that the perception of *red* light is diminished or less sensitive and can be confused. *Protanopia* means that no red light is perceived at all; the red segment of the colour spectrum cannot be seen at all. People with Protanopia, known as *Protanopes,* will be missing or have no function from their red cone. People with Protanomaly, known as *Protanomalous,* will have their red cone but it will be faulty or out of alignment.

Deuteranomaly means that the perception of *green* light is diminished or less sensitive and can be confused. Known as *Deuteranomalous,* these people will be trichromatic anomalous and have all cones, but their green cone will be faulty or out of alignment. *Deuteranopia* means that no green light is perceived at all; the green segment of the colour spectrum cannot be seen at all. Known as *Deuteranopes*, these people will be missing or have no function from their green cone. For example, I am deuteranomalous because I have difficulty distinguishing between green, yellow and orange colours.

Finally, *Tritanomaly* means that the perception of *blue* light is diminished or less sensitive and can be confused. Known as *Tritanomalous,* these people will be anomalous trichromats and have all cones but their blue cone will be faulty or out of alignment. *Tritanopia* means that no blue light is perceived at all; the blue segment of the colour spectrum cannot be seen at all. Known as *Tritanopes,* these people will be missing or have no function from their blue cone. Tritanomaly and Tritanopia are also known as *blue-yellow* colour blindness.

Red-green colour blindness, the most common variation, is either Protanomaly and Deuteranomaly or Protanopia and Deuteranopia.

Here is a table to make these variations easier to understand:

Variation of condition	Problems	Trichromatic?	Colour affected
Protanomaly	Faulty or out-of-alignment green cone	Yes	Red
Protanopia	Green cone missing or dysfunctional	No	Red
Deuteranomaly	Faulty or out-of-alignment red cone	Yes	Green
Deuteranopia	Red cone missing or dysfunctional	No	Green
Tritanomaly	Faulty or out-of-alignment blue cone	Yes	Blue
Tritanopia	Blue cone missing or dysfunctional	No	Blue

See how I organised the table using colour? It was a bit of a challenge and I'm still not sure if the colours are correct. If you are unable to see any green writing, you're probably a deuteranope.

These different groups of people will therefore confuse different sets of colour. Their colour blindness isn't limited solely to the colour perceived by the cone that is deficient. The following lists will outline the various colours confused by those with each variation:

Protanopes confuse:

- Black with red.
- Dark brown with dark green, dark orange and dark red.
- Blues with red, purple and pink.
- Mid-green with orange.

Deuteranopes confuse:

- Mid-green with mid-red.
- Blueish-green/turquoise with mid-pink and grey.
- Yellow with bright "lime" green.
- Light grey with light pink.
- Mid-brown with mid-red.
- Lilac with light blue.

Tritanopes confuse:

> - Grey with light blue.
> - Dark purple with black.
> - Red and orange.
> - Mid-green and blue.
> - Dark purple with black.

As mentioned before, Monochromacy is almost like grey-scale vision. However, like Trichromacy and Dichromacy, there are variations in this type of colour blindness. *Cone Monochromacy* is a failure of two of the three cone cells. There is red, green and blue Cone Monochromacy. As the brain needs to compare information from more than one cone to perceive colour, those with Cone Monochromacy are unable to distinguish between all colours.

Rod Monochromacy (Achromatopsia) is the rarest and most severe form of colour blindness. Rod Monochromacy means that none of the cone cells are functional. This means that no colours can be seen at all – the world is seen in black, white and grey. Since rods respond to dim light, people with this condition are also very sensitive to bright lights.

The most common method used for diagnosing colour blindness is the *Ishihara* test, named after the Japanese scientist who invented it. The test was invented in 1918 and used for military medical assessments. The test uses many small coloured circles to conceal patterns which include hidden numbers. The circles that form the numbers are coloured differently to the rest of the circles. However, colour blind people are unable to see the difference between the two colours. Most of the tests are red and green with some being blue and yellow and a small number incorporating oranges and pinks.

Though not incredibly common, colour blindness affects a larger proportion of the population than you'd think. About 1 in 12 men are colour blind in the UK and this is similar worldwide. This varies between different sources; some say that the estimate should be closer to 1 in 10 men. The 1 in 12 figure was taken from *colourblindawareness.org.* It is estimated that about 1 in 200 women are colour blind; and that the condition in women is usually less severe. These figures equate to roughly 2.7 million people in the UK being colour blind – about 4.5% of the population.

When comparing the number of colour blind people worldwide it is slightly more complicated. There is limited research and the figures are not exact but data shows that the condition is more common amongst white (Caucasian), European men. For example, the average percentage of colour blind men in any country is about 8%. However, it is 11-12% of men in Scandinavia. Furthermore the condition is less prevalent amongst Sub-Saharan African men.

The variation continues with different types of colour blindness. Though it is much harder to make comparisons about female colour blindness, as far fewer women have the condition, there is a lot of variation amongst men. Out of the 8% of men, worldwide, that are colour blind:

- 1% are *Deuteranopes*.
- 1% are *Protanopes*.
- 1% are *Protanomalous*.
- 5% are *Deuteranomalous*.
- 1 in 30-50,000 are *Tritanopes/Tritanomalous*.
- About 3% are affected due to age/medical issues.
- About 50% have *mild* anomalous deficiency.

Red-green colour blindness is the most common amongst both men and women. Most women with the condition are usually anomalous trichromats.

Colour blindness is mostly present at birth and remains for life. However, some may contract the condition with old age or with other illnesses. This can also lead to other problems. For example, most people that are born with the conditions will have the same effect for both eyes. However, when contracted with age, the effects can differ for each eye. A decline in general vision can also be associated with contracted colour blindness.

Though sometimes age related, contracted colour blindness can be a product of an injury or disease. Certain diseases, such as *Alzheimer's* and *Parkinson's*, increase the risk of contracting colour blindness. The use of some drugs, for example *Hydroxychloroquine* – used to treat rheumatism, can also increase the risk of contracting the condition. Damage to the *retina* or *optic nerve* is also a common cause of contracted colour blindness.

It is therefore quite clear that colour blindness is much more complicated than simply being unable to see certain colours; and that it can manifest itself in many different ways.

CHAPTER 2: EVERYDAY PROBLEMS FACED BY COLOUR BLIND PEOPLE

This chapter will be split into sections to make it easier to compare the different challenges.

Food

Food is very important in our daily lives and vital for energy and survival, of course. Many would think that, for colour blind people food is not a problem at all – they buy it, eat it and it gives them energy to continue with their day. For some foods this is true but it is little things which make a difference.

The top three tomatoes are green, and the rest are red. If you are unable to see the green ones, you are a protanope and if you are unable to see the red ones you are a deuteranope. I can tell the difference but to me the red ones are more brown.

Ripeness is important, not only for taste but sometimes for health – eat an out-of-date piece of fruit and you could be in for a long night of stomach pains. This can be a great challenge for colour blind people. Take bananas, for example. A ripe banana will be bright yellow and an under-ripe one will be a greenish colour. I didn't discover that I was colour blind until I was 15 and this problem suddenly made sense. Even before I knew I was colour blind, I always found it hard to tell if a banana was ripe and often asked my mother. Rather than using the colour to tell if a banana was ripe, I would make a judgement by looking at the number of black spots on the fruit, as this can sometimes indicate ripeness.

The problem extends beyond bananas. Many fruits and vegetables change colour as they ripen. Tomatoes change from green to red – a nightmare for a gardener who is red-green colour blind. The same goes for strawberries. Even choosing apples can be difficult as green and red apples have different flavours and textures which are preferred by different people. Though apples will have names on the packaging if purchased in a supermarket, picking from an apple tree or from a farm shop could be quite difficult for a colour blind person.

The ripeness issue then extends to the other end of the spectrum – out-of-date produce. Take an ordinarily looking healthy salad, full of ripe green vegetables. For someone with severe red-green colour blindness, it will be hard to see the bright green colours of a ripe vegetable or fruit. Instead, the colour could be interpreted as diminished or even grey; which could suggest mould. This could lead to colour blind people wasting good, ripe food and in essence wasting money.

If you're not colour blind, you might have an easy time picking items when you go shopping. If items are colour coded for flavour, you'll easily be able to distinguish between them and swiftly pick up a product without taking a second glance. For example, strawberry-flavoured products are often red and raspberry-flavoured products a pinkish colour, so I am told. This is a difficult to spot for colour blind people and can mean that they need to take time choosing between products. It sounds like a very small inconvenience but if you added up everything you bought during a shop and had to take time choosing even just a few products, the time you spend shopping would be increased. Remember those trusty bananas that I just spoke about – choosing ripe produce can be another hard, time consuming part of shopping for colour blind people.

Food problems extend beyond the shops. What do you often do with food once you've bought it? Cook it, of course! Most people find following a recipe and preparing a meal fairly easy if they have basic cooking skills and know their way around a kitchen. This, again, is a very simple everyday task that most of us find easy. Not for colour blind people, however.

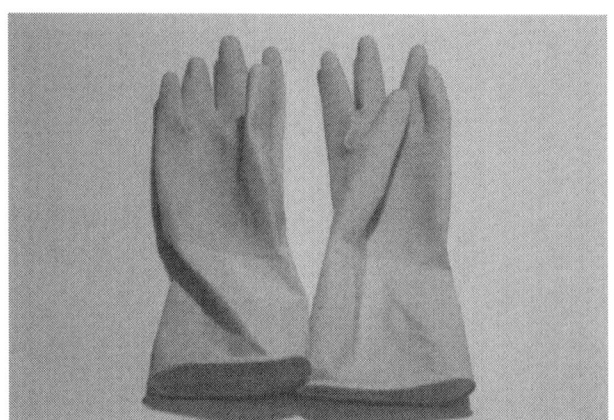

For the washing up, which colour are these 'marigolds' to you? People with normal vision will see yellow, but I see green.

Take cooking a nice, juicy, tender steak for a Friday night treat. Most people will pop it on the pan for a few minutes and remove it when it's red in the middle and pink on the outside. Spotted the problem yet? The problem is that colour blind people often confuse pink and red. So, they might either think the steak is pink too soon, remove it from the pan, eat it rare and spend the night with chronic stomach pain. On the other hand, they might see it as red for too long and have a tough, dry dinner. As someone who loves a rare steak, the latter would be a huge disappointment indeed.

The yogurt pot on the left is more red and is strawberry

flavour. The one on the right is more pink and is raspberry flavour. I can tell the difference but need to look for a good few seconds before deciphering which one is which.

What about a nice, healthy stir fry if you're on a diet? Easy, right? Well, most people will chuck all their ingredients in a pan for a few minutes and voilà. Colour blind people, however, will run into many spots of bother. Usually green peppers taste best cooked and are more commonly eaten cooked than red, yellow and orange peppers. Imagine the dilemma, you're red-green colour blind, you reach for a pepper from your shelves, you can't tell whether it's a green or red one but you pick it, slice it and chuck it in the pan. Oh snap! It's a red one. So now you'll have a less flavoursome red pepper in your stir fry; and a bitter, raw green pepper for your crudités in your packed lunch. First-world problems, I know; but it's another simple issue faced by colour blind people that's so small but equally so infuriating on a day-to-day basis.

Finally, cooking can often require judgement by eye – like cooking the steak. For example, if you bake a loaf of bread, you'll be told to take it out not after an exact measurement of time, but when it looks "golden brown on top." Most will easily follow this instruction, but for colour blind people – many of whom cannot differ between brown and yellow, for example – they'll be stood over their oven asking themselves whether they should chance it and take out a loaf that could be either too soggy or too dry. It's simple, again, and not a great issue but it's still infuriating for a colour blind person that just wants to make themselves a nice loaf of bread.

So, it is quite clear that there are many small things, and some larger ones, that can alter a colour blind person's experience with food. Not only is this no fun when they want to cook a perfect meal; but it can sometimes be a health risk if they can't tell if raw meat is cooked well enough.

Clothing

I'm not going to say that I'm at all a fashion guru or someone who's really that bothered about what I wear.

However, I do know how important it is to look smart and presentable – not just at work but in everyday life. Many people are conscious about matching their clothing items so that they look the part. This sometimes consists of either matching colours or shades, or choosing colours that complement each other; for example red and green.

Colour blind people may find it hard to either match colours or select colours that complement each other. For example, red-green colour blind people will not see red and green properly. Depending on the severity of their condition, they might see the two colours as pink and yellow. Can you imagine a pink and yellow outfit?

I put that shirt on thinking that it was blue and wore it

to school. Everyone said that it was purple. How embarrassing!

This other shirt looks pink to me, but everyone tells me

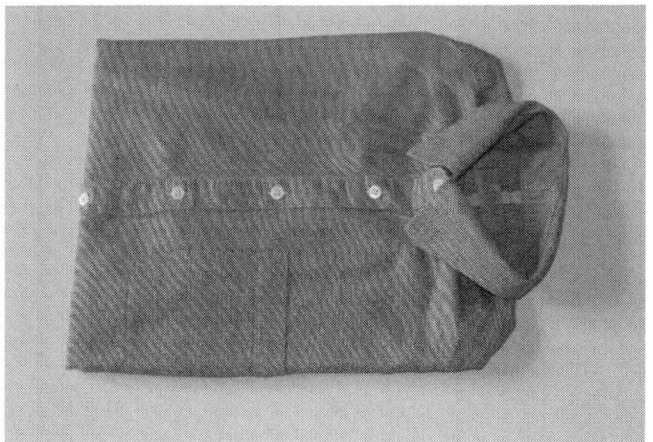

that it is red. Once again, I wore it to school but the colour was not brought up.

The same goes for people that are blue-yellow colour blind. Blue and yellow complement each other fairly well and are used in many logo combinations. However, someone who is blue-yellow colour blind may see these colours as lilac and turquoise – an interesting combination for sure!

The issue extends beyond choosing colours that complement each other well, what about matching colours and shades? Say you just bought a red t-shirt, or one that looked red despite your colour blindness. Wouldn't it be nice to find a red baseball cap that matched your t-shirt? Well, this could be an issue. If you can't see reds properly, you'll have trouble matching the colours. You could end up with a blood-red t-shirt and a strawberry-coloured hat. This isn't the end of the world, but it doesn't look as smart as having the two colours matched.

It's strange because I have subconsciously stayed away from red and green clothing, as I am red-green colour blind. Most of my t-shirts are grey and blue. Of course, many people tend not to wear bright red and green clothes regularly; but it is quite interesting how I seem to subconsciously stray away from colours that I am unsure about.

Another clothing issue for colour blind people is stains. Stains are very annoying! It always seems to be that you spill coffee down your brand-new t-shirt. Depending on the colour of your item of clothing and the colour of the substance you stained yourself with, you should normally be able to spot a darker patch where the item of clothing is stained. However, once the stain has dried it may become less obvious. An example could be a stain from strawberries. Say, for example, you spill some strawberry juice on your new pink t-shirt (great choice of colour). People who are not colour blind would be able to see the subtle difference between the colour of the t-shirt and the colour of the stain.

However, those with the condition may be unable to separate the two shades – they may not even see the t-shirt as pink for a start! This could be embarrassing and is very frustrating for colour blind people.

Yet again, though these issues are small and seem insignificant, they can sometimes be really frustrating for colour blind people as they deal with them every day.

Work

Like food, work is VERY important and is something that we all engage in on a day-to-day basis. Even children, who are at school, are technically working as they are doing tasks that require cognitive input and result in a certain outcome – unfortunately, unlike their adult counter parts, the outcome is not money.

It's clear that work is important, and this is also true for colour blind people. However, along with the usual stresses and strains experienced by everyone at work, colour blind people have to deal with many more small issues that make their lives a little bit harder every day. Though colour blind people are unable to pursue many careers, even the jobs they can do often provide difficulties for them.

There are many different issues for colour blind people in the work place but let's start with technology. Computers are now something that most of us will use at some point in our working lives. One programme that features on computers is *Microsoft Word.* This is a word processor that makes typing emails, reports and many more important things a breeze; almost. The boffins at Microsoft even thought of an easy way to ensure that your work is grammatically correct. This consists of red, green and blue lines that underline any misspelt or grammatically incorrect words and phrases. Brilliant - unless you're colour blind. Though you'll be able to tamper with your language until something fits correctly, it can be frustrating not knowing whether the issue is a spelling error (red line); or grammatical error (green line).

This helpfully leads me on to the next interesting thing I have noticed about my colour blindness – it's worse with computers. Normally I can tell the difference between a bright red and bright green fairly easily. For some reason, this becomes much harder when I use a programme like *Word*. This also becomes much harder when viewing items on a screen; an example being when I can distinguish between green and yellow lights in real life but find it more challenging when viewed on TV or a computer.

Another common thing many of us will use at work is a presentation or chart of statistics. Take most bar graphs and pie charts and they'll all have different colours for their bars of segments. As you've probably guessed, this is a big issue for colour blind people. Not only does it make it harder to interpret data, but it also makes presenting it harder and can often become more time consuming than it should be.

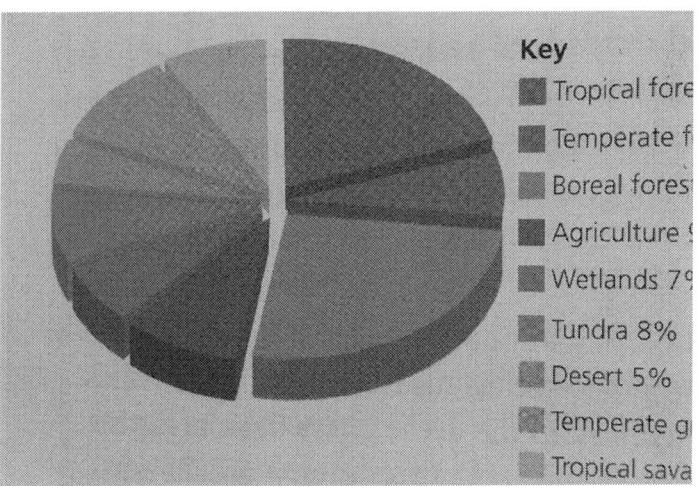

Here is an example of a pie chart that I found in my geography textbook. As you may be able to see, there are greens and reds next to each other and also blues next to each other. I must say that matching some of these colours to the key is a little tricky; particularly the blue/purple colours.

Coloured pens and pencils may sound a little childish, but in the work place they are more common than you would think. Take a jobs or task roster for different groups. If you're in green group but you can't see your colour on the roster correctly, you may end up accidentally doing the work for red group.

This extends to using colour to organise things. Filing cabinets may use coloured files as a way of organising various items or documents. This is also common in concertina files – each section will be marked with a coloured tab. An inability to see this may end up in documents being incorrectly filed, which will lead to an unhappy boss and a disheartened employee.

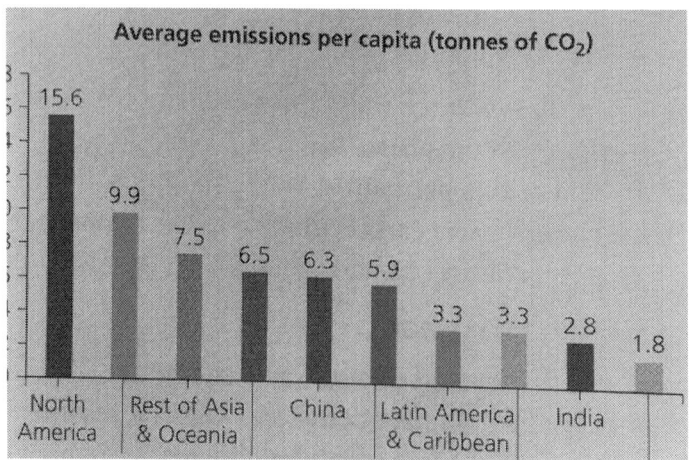

Here is a bar graph that I found. Though you can make sense of the graph without the colours, it is still frustrating being unable to tell the difference. I am struggling to distinguish between the purple/blue bars.

Possibly the most interesting work issue would be marketing or design. Brands' labels and logos are often very colourful but also often use harmonious or contrasting colours. If you are colour blind and cannot see this, you may create a logo that's not as striking as it could be because you can't tell if the colours go well together.

There are, of course, many solutions for all of these problems which will be mentioned later on in the book; but it's still fascinating to discover all of the tiny areas of life that can be affected by colour blindness.

Leisure

Obviously, leisure is a vast topic that can extend to all corners of life. Therefore, I won't mention every little issue that colour blind people could face when going about their free time – it would need about a thousand pages and would probably bore you to death. Instead, in this section I will include some of my own experiences as someone who is red-green colour blind.

One of the first times that I had difficulty with distinguishing between colours was go-karting. Many of you will be familiar with the red, yellow and green flags used to make racing safer. When I went go-karting, everyone was told that a red flag meant return to the pits immediately, a yellow flag meant stop where you were on the track and a green flag meant resume racing. Failure to adhere to these rules would result in disqualification and no fun at all. I remember seeing a flag which I thought was yellow and stopping. I waited, but when I saw the next flag I was unable to tell if it was green or yellow. I ended up holding everyone up and this was rather embarrassing. Imagine if it was the other way around, though, if I'd ignored the yellow flag because I thought it was green. Not only would I have been disqualified but I could have ended up causing a crash – Pastor Maldonado and Daniil Kvyat would have been proud!

The next story comes from a holiday at the beach – how lovely! Normally, you go in the sea and have a lot of fun. However, in France, they're quite namby-pamby about what you're allowed to do at the beach. They use flags to inform you about the sea. Green means all clear, time to have fun; yellow means swimming is ok but keep young children and inflatables away; red means it's too dangerous to swim and purple means the water is polluted – i.e. swim at your peril. I remember taking the rubber dinghy into the sea with my brother. Both of us are red-green colour blind and so we saw the flag from afar and thought that it was green. A few moments later, we had a rather bossy French lifeguard shooing us out of the sea. Doing my best to talk to the smarty pants lifeguard, I asked if I could swim without the boat and sulked away into the sea. Yet again, this was rather embarrassing.

This colour-coding nightmare continued at the swimming pool one Saturday. The pool uses coloured wristbands to tell you how long you have in the pool. After an hour or so, they'll say: "orange wristband holders please leave the pool." Rather unfriendly but I suppose that's how they make their money. What annoyed me was that the wrist bands weren't very clear. Rather than being black and white, they were orange, gold and yellow. This was painfully hard for me. When: "orange wristbands please leave the pool," rang out of the speaker, I glared long and hard at the wristband on my wrist. I decided that the band was closer to yellow than orange and decided to remain in the water. Five minutes later I was shouted at by a grouchy life guard and told to leave. I did so but this was rather embarrassing as I had everyone staring at my brother and me as we left the pool.

A final point that occurred to me was blood in urine. Urine is usually green or yellow and blood usually red. If you're a protanope you won't be able to see the blood if you have a problem. This could pose serious issues if you have a kidney problem that needs checking out.

That concludes this chapter. There are some issues that I purposefully left out as they link to other chapters. Read on to find them.

CHAPTER 3 – COLOUR BLINDNESS AND EDUCATION

Education is really, really important for us all. From the age of four, when we all start school, right up until the age of 16-18. Without basic education, children have no hopes of getting a job and becoming independent. This is well known by teachers, schools and the government; and so every effort is made to accommodate children with disabilities or difficulties, right? Well, many with more obvious conditions receive help, but for colour blind people the story can be different.

It is thought that roughly 80% of colour blind children are undiagnosed when they start school and that many will remain undiagnosed well into their teens. I, for example, was not diagnosed until the age of 15. This doesn't mean that it can't be hard for undiagnosed children. In fact, it can be very challenging. Diagnosed children will understand their condition and will be able to inform their teachers of any difficulties. Those who are not diagnosed may become confused and even stressed when they find performing simple tasks more difficult than their peers.

Problems faced by colour blind children at school

When I began researching this section, I thought that issues would only arise in primary school when colour is used to engage children in their lessons. I was wrong; colour can be prevalent across all stages of learning and can have big impacts on a student's performance.

Starting with primary school, the more obvious issues are easy to relate to. Take colour coding, for example. Teachers may instruct students to organise paper, pencils, books or other equipment into colour-coded boxes for storage. For example, plain paper may be stored in a red box and lined paper in a green one. A colour blind child may have difficulty in telling the boxes apart and may have to look harder to identify the correct box. Alternatively, the student may require assistance from a peer or teacher. This can be humiliating for young children; especially if they have little knowledge about their condition.

This issue also extends to coloured pens and pencils, which are used across all school years. There is the classic scenario where it's tidy-up time and students must return all of their pencils to the correct section of the tray. Often these trays have many shades or reds, greens, browns, blues and yellows. If you remember my lists from chapter one, you'll know that these colours are often confused. Teachers are often very harsh on children who put pencils in the wrong box and peers can become frustrated too. This can be stressful and humiliating for colour blind children.

I have my own story for this topic. I always find it particularly hard to differ between red, brown and dark green pencils. Sometimes I even confuse black with dark green. Once, I couldn't tell if a pencil was dark green or black. I asked a friend to pass me the black one. When it was time to return the pencil, I didn't know where to place it as I couldn't distinguish between the colours. So I just placed it in the nearest slot. Later that day, the teacher told us to put the pencils away correctly and other students complained about the misplacing of pencils. I was 10 at the time and unaware of my condition, but nevertheless I felt humiliated for my error.

Here are some coloured pencils. Top left are purple, bottom left are blue, top middle are red, bottom middle are brown, top right are green and bottom right are yellow. I am unable to differ between yellow and green, some of the reds with some of the browns and some of the purple with some of the blues. I have trouble

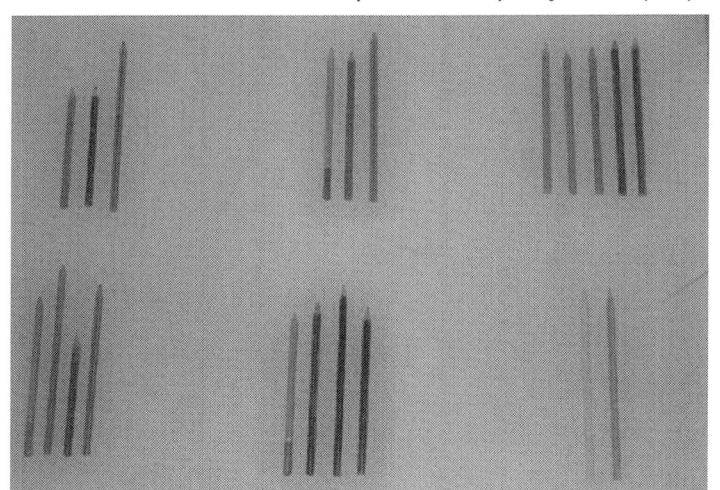

splitting the different shades of brown the most. What about you?

A nursery school problem that can be quite hard to deal with is learning colours. All children will be told that the grass is green and that the sky is blue. Colour blind children will follow this in their naivety, even if the grass looks brown to them. This can be problematic in the future when they have to identify something that is green, but actually see it as brown. This occurred to me very recently I remember the optician telling me that I would be able to pick up colour that I cannot see because I will have been told what colour things are throughout my life by colour-able people. I was walking along one day when I looked at the road side and suddenly realised that double-yellow lines appear green to me. Of course, I had been told that they were yellow all my life and had gone along with this. Still, it is interesting to see what I see when I am not told what colour something is. Now that I have been diagnosed, I am making new discoveries every day. Another example is traffic lights. I have been told for all my life that they are red, amber and green. However, when I look closely they appear blue, green and orange to me.

Problems continue in secondary school, particularly in maths. Students will learn about ratio and proportion and a common exercise for this is separating red and green counters into groups and determining the ratio. However, colour blind children will struggle to tell the difference and will therefore take more time to grasp the skill. Having this difficulty is also frustrating for a child when their peers find the task easy.

Remember when I said that my colour blindness is worse on a screen? Well, many schools now use websites for homework tasks. I used various maths websites for my homework. Some of the tasks were made more difficult due to my colour blindness. For example, a task that used bar graphs was made more difficult as I struggled to tell the difference between reds, greens and yellows. This meant I had to re-do the assignment; which made me frustrated and worsened my concentration.

The chart issues extend to other subject, for example geography. Geography is known as a subject that involves lot of colouring in and interpreting data from graphs. A common example is colouring in population densities in a map. Use a darker shade of red or green for an area with a greater population. This is very hard for a colour blind student and their work can often turn out to be completely wrong. They may have to re-do the work, which is very frustrating; especially if the work is to be re-done at a break or as additional homework.

I think this has to be the most ridiculous data

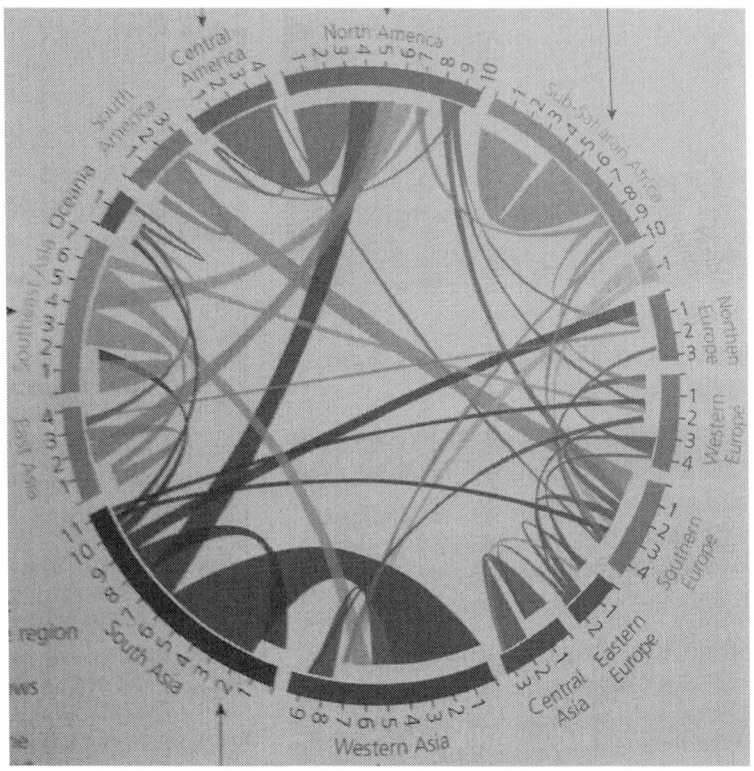

presentation method I have ever come across! I have not yet covered it in class but I think it has something to do with migration or trade. Not only is it difficult to see the where the lines go; it is impossible to see the colours. The whole of the right side looks virtually the same colour to me and even some of the left side looks really similar.

I fell victim to the coloured charts in my geography GCSE paper. The question involved selecting the area of the country with the lowest rain fall. Each area was shaded in green; darker green meant lower rain fall. I had to look long and hard before making a choice, I even considered asking an invigilator for help at one point. There was a separate room for colour blind children where they would receive help on the colour-coded questions. The reason I was not included was that I was not diagnosed until I was 15 and half-way through secondary school; meaning my medical notes had not been updated. So I suppose it's my own fault – a lesson to all of you whom have up-coming exams.

This is not quite the same as the rainfall map in the

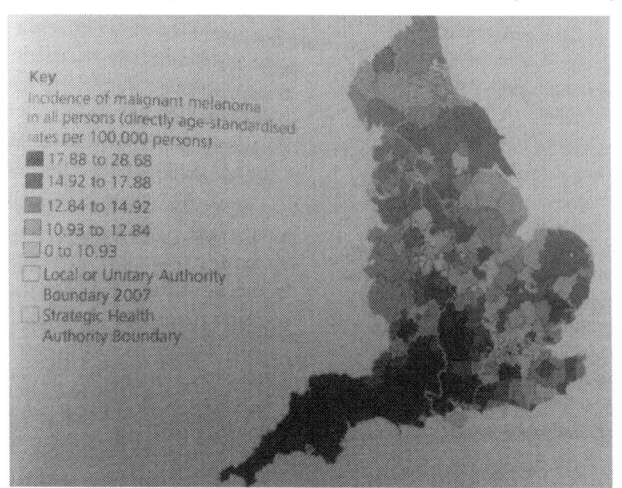

Key
Incidence of malignant melanoma
in all persons (directly age-standardised
rates per 100,000 persons)
17.88 to 28.68
14.92 to 17.88
12.84 to 14.92
10.93 to 12.84
0 to 10.93
Local or Unitary Authority Boundary 2007
Strategic Health Authority Boundary

exam but the colour scheme and size of the map are very similar. I am unable to distinguish between the two darkest and two medium shades and two lightest shades. Essentially, this means that I can only see three categories; rather than six.

Finally, there is the issue of art and design, where colour can be hugely important. A task may require students to use certain colours to paint a picture. If the student uses the incorrect colours they may feel humiliated and get marked down. Something I found very hard was colour mixing and shading. The class was instructed to mix certain colours to make a new shade. In order to make darker and lighter variations of the colour, we would have to mix different ratios of the primary colours. I was hopeless and each of my variations looked the same in my eyes. Again, this was at the age of 13 and so I was still undiagnosed. It was frustrating for me being told by my friends or the teacher that my work was not varied enough.

What is already done to help colour blind pupils

Though there are many ways in which colour blind pupils are held back, there are some things that have been done to help them. Possibly the most obvious is labelling coloured pencils. Each pencil will have a label wrapped around the top of it that clearly states the colour of that pencil. This means pupils need not spend ages deciding which colour it is or having to ask fellow peers. This is easy and costs nothing to do, so it is sometimes surprising when some schools do not use this aid.

Using a similar idea, some schools may apply labels to boxes and shelves; whether they contain coloured items or simply use colours to organise things. Once again this is very easy and prevents a colour blind pupil placing an object in the wrong place or having to ask a peer.

Colour-coding systems can be very useful and effective, but obviously a nightmare for colour blind children. Though colour-coding systems are very easy to use, there are other just as easy and effective methods that don't discriminate against colour blind pupils. For example, using letters and numbers for groups rather than colours is easy; or for very young children patterns and shapes can be just as useful. Again, these methods are very easy to use and do not discriminate against colour blind pupils.

These are just a few examples of how the education system has tried to adapt itself for colour blind children; but there is still a long way to go. Teachers and teaching assistants need more awareness of the condition and need to know basic methods that colour blind children can use to compensate for their issues. Furthermore, schools need to put less emphasis on learning with colours for young children – numbers, letters and even patterns are just as simple to use.

Alarming facts

Ok, so you've just learned a fair bit about the difficulties faced by colour blind children in education, but there are more facts which are slightly more alarming than the previous ones in this chapter. These facts really did surprise me, and they might surprise you too.

I just told you how teachers need to know more about colour blindness in order to help pupils with the condition. Well, it's a true fact that almost all teachers have no knowledge and certainly aren't trained to deal with those affected. Those that do have some knowledge likely have family members or friends with the condition.

This is a big problem; as I have already mentioned to an extent. If teachers do not know how to help a colour blind child, the child could end up underperforming and having to work harder than other pupils, which can be stressful and tiring for them. Furthermore, children will feel that they have nobody to talk to if the condition is making their learning more difficult and as a result may feel excluded. This can sometimes even lead to mental health issues.

Another saddening fact is that many of the educational resources available to children, such as text books and websites, can be challenging to use for colour blind children. Coloured illustrations can become meaningless and interactive educational games that use colours can be much harder for children with the condition. Websites can be particularly problematic because colour blindness can often be worse on screens.

This, again, can have terrible consequences. Children that struggle to use colour-themed games and activities can become frustrated and stressed and homework tasks that use colour may have to be taken again; meaning that children have to work unnecessarily harder. Once again, this can lead to mental health issues and can be detrimental to a child's progress.

Perhaps the most alarming fact is that very few children are screened – 80% of colour blind children leave school undiagnosed. This means that many school children will be struggling and not know how to cope. If children are screened, they can learn to cope with their condition and can inform teachers of it; so that they understand the reason behind any colour related difficulties. If children do not know that they are colour blind, they can become stressed and the everyday struggles can build up and lead to mental health issues.

Why colour blind children need more help

In case you hadn't already noticed, the issue of colour blindness can run deeper than you thought. What might have been a small everyday issue could have turned into a mental health issue.

As with any other difficulty, colour blindness can lead to underperforming and hardship in school. The lack of awareness and the alarming lack of screening can lead to colour blind children dropping out of school early. The problem gets worse with mental health issues. Any children with mental health issues will find school harder that other children; and mental health issues as a result of the repercussions of a lack of awareness of colour blindness are no different.

As I mentioned before, if a child finds a task more challenging due to their colour blindness, they will become frustrated and more stressed than those around them. Having to work harder may put more pressure on them and even make them feel more of an outsider when they are unable to enjoy colour-themed activities with other children. Too much stress can lead to anxiety and can become a serious mental health issue.

Furthermore, if children are failing tasks due to their condition, they may lose motivation and thus underperform. Underperformance can lead to increased pressure, humiliation and can cause a great deal of sadness. These can once again lead to mental health issues and can result in dropping out.

All of these issues could be rectified to a great extent by simply raising awareness about colour blindness and providing more help for children with the condition. The problem is easier to solve than it seems.

An interesting note that I'll add is that the problems faced by colour blind children at school are almost like a rabbit hole – they can go much, much deeper than expected. This links to the mental health issue – a child could easily become suicidal if they find out that they can't pursue their dream job due to their condition. Although it seems extreme, it is a very real possibility and is evidence that the problem can have consequences that are much worse than expected.

CHAPTER 4 - COLOUR BLINDNESS AND CAREERS

This, for the younger readers or parents, is probably the chapter that you ought to pay attention to most. So far, the book has been composed mostly of useful, but not vital, information about colour blindness. This chapter, however, is really quite important. Careers take up huge amounts of our lives and most of us devote 40+ years of our lives to that career. Of course, people often have career changes. However, interestingly, most of the careers affected by colour blindness are careers that people are passionate about or usually keep for life.

So, without further ado, here are some of the major careers that colour blind people will unfortunately miss out on.

Airline pilot

I listed airline pilot first not only because it is a major career, but also because it was the career that I wanted to follow before I was diagnosed. Though I had flown on a plane when I was about 9 months old, my first real trip on a plane was in May 2017 when I was 15 years old. From the moment the jets spooled up for take-off to the crash of the landing gear touching down, I became in-love with aviation. I immediately researched how to become a pilot.

I had done all the research and had even installed plane simulators; I had become rather obsessed with aviation. I was prepared to work for a position as a pilot. However, in August 2017, a mere 3 months after my passion for aviation had begun, I was diagnosed. Though I wasn't immediately aware that I would be unable to fly, when I researched the career further I discovered that I would most likely be unable to fly.

Though you can get a private pilot's license to fly light aircraft during the day and land at small airports, you'll be lucky to become a professional. Most colour blindness is unacceptable in commercial aviation as pilots must obtain a first-class medical certificate to become a professional pilot; and you won't achieve a first-class medical certificate if you are colour blind.

Though the Civil Aviation Authority will give you an opportunity to become a pilot if you have mild colour anomalies with a lantern test; most operators won't give you a seat if you don't have a first-class medical. For example, I once came across an advertisement for a job at Aer Lingus when I was researching the career. There were virtually no entry requirements, apart from one thing: perfect colour vision.

Flying private jets is possible with a second-class medical, but the authorities will still require near-perfect colour vision and you would probably have to take a lantern test. This means that only a small percentage of colour blind people would have a chance.

The reason that colour blindness is forbidden in commercial aviation is firstly due to the nature of the job. As a pilot, you share responsibility of hundreds of lives with one other pilot and have to safely operate a multi-million pound jet. For this reason, aviation companies want their pilots to be in perfect health. Other conditions, such as diabetes can also be forbidden in aviation.

Another reason that colour blindness is not allowed in aviation is because the systems that pilots and airports use include colours. PaPi lights, used for landing, use red and green signals to keep an aircraft on a safe glideslope. Failure to see these signals correctly could result in an unsafe landing. Navigation lights are also red and green on aircraft wings. Pilots must be able to see red and green clearly so that they can determine the direction that a nearby aircraft is travelling in. Taxi lines and lights at airports are also yellow/orange; so good colour vision is preferable.

Air traffic controller

Air traffic controllers need to be able to use similar colour-coded systems to pilots, so they obviously need good colour vision. However, colour vision is perhaps even more necessary for air traffic controllers than pilots because they need to be able to see different coloured icons on screens. This is even more important because many colour blind people find their condition worsens when using screens. Combine this with the fact that air traffic controllers are responsible for far more people than pilots, and it's clear to see why good colour vision is even more important for them.

Train driver/railway engineer/conductor/guard

Train driver is probably the most well-known career for being out of reach of colour blind people. Train drivers need to be able to clearly see red and green lights from a long distance away so that they can stop the train if necessary. They also use other red, yellow and green signals at stations, sidings and in communication with other railway workers. As you have probably guessed, perfect colour vision is absolutely mandatory; and the restrictions are even more stringent than in the aviation industry. Though trains are not as advanced as planes, train drivers are still responsible for the lives of many people.

Railway engineers must also be able to see the same signals as train drivers for safe maintenance of the railways. Though they are not responsible for the lives of many passengers, they must work around very dangerous equipment in a safe and orderly fashion. Thus, perfect colour vision is considered a necessity as a safety measure. Once again, the rules are very tight and there will be no exceptions; even for people with mild colour anomalies.

Conductors are as responsible for safe operation of the train as the driver and must also use many red, yellow and green signals to co-operate safely with their driver. In fact, they can hold more responsibility for reacting to colour signals from guards when leaving the station. The medical test will be virtually identical to that of a train driver and will require the same high standard of colour vision. The same applies for the guards, who have a very similar role on the platform.

Put plainly, you will unfortunately not be allowed to work anywhere near a railway if you have colour blindness in the UK. This is actually quite a significant career as it is the dream of many young boys, my younger self included, to drive trains. Breaking the news to a young child that has just been diagnosed can be truly heart breaking.

Electrician

Another career infamous for being out of reach for colour blind people is that of an electrician. It's the cliché of "make sure you cut the green wire; if you cut the red one a fire will start." Though this is an old-fashioned cliché, it is quite accurate. Electricians often have to deal with coloured wires and have to be able to work with them safely. Not only can their job be fairly dangerous, as electricity can kill; they are also responsible for keeping their client's home in good order – a mistake that results in a fire could lead to thousands of pounds worth of damage.

However, these days the differences between the colours of the wires are much clearer and will be no problem for most colour blind people. It is possible to become a domestic electrician if you are colour blind, though you'll have to self-fund your training as apprentices must pass a colour vision test. Careers in the forces and on some commercial levels are still likely to be out of reach as they carry more responsibility and can involve more wires and therefore more colours.

Firefighter

I was quite surprised when I found out that firefighters couldn't be colour blind. I obviously knew that fires could be different colours and that it may be useful to be able to distinguish; but I didn't think that it was a make-or-break thing.

The main reasons that good colour vision is important are for identifying industrial gas cylinders, road signs, the colours on portable extinguishers and pieces of firefighting equipment. A D15 test is the mandatory test for entry, but applicants must also clear an Ishihara test. As with the test for electricians, some mildly deuteranomalous people may be able to reach the standards.

Doctor/medical practitioner/pharmacists

In general, most colour blind people should be able to receive a basic license for medical practice. However, colour vision can be important in certain strains of medicine for reading scans, performing operations and visually diagnosing. For example, colour blind people may struggle to see rashes or abnormal discolouration, which could lead to an incorrect diagnosis.

Furthermore, surgeons need good colour vision to be able to perform safe operations. For example, they need to be able to see that blood is a healthy colour.

Similar issues apply to pharmacists, who need to be able to identify the correct colour of certain medication in order to practice safely.

As I mentioned before, colour blindness is not a complete barrier to a career in medicine; but may throw up some obstacles along the way. Those whose condition is more severe may have more issues than those with mild anomalies.

Lorry driver

Yet another surprising career is that of lorry driver. You would think that if you're allowed to drive a car; you'd be allowed to driver a lorry. The reasons are as follows: lorry drivers are expected to have excellent vision for safe operation of their vehicles. As haulage companies are businesses, they don't want to hire someone who may be more of a liability to their company than most people. The chance of an accident involving the incorrect perception of colours increases your liability to the company.

Furthermore, as lorries are tall vehicles, traffic lights may sometimes be more difficult to see and the lights could be mixed from an obscure angle.

Finally, safe operation of large vehicles extends beyond simple traffic lights. Lorry drivers could have to follow colour signals when manoeuvring in a yard or they may have to tell the difference between different coloured goods. There are more reasons than you would think.

An Ishihara test is likely to be mandatory for acquiring an HGV license, so the rules are stricter than some occupations where mild anomalies are acceptable.

Chef

You could become a self-employed chef with colour blindness, but it is hard to land a job or apprenticeship with the condition. The reasons are clear; colour plays a big part in judging ripeness of fruit and vegetable and whether meat is past-its-best. Colour can also be important in cooking - a perfect steak may be pink, not red; and if you're colour blind you'll have trouble telling if the meat is red or pink.

Furthermore, it is important to be *good* at cooking if you want to be a chef. Overcooking a steak at home is no biggie, but in a restaurant your customers won't be pleased and neither will your boss.

The rules aren't that clear, so if you want to be a chef talk to some apprenticeship providers and see what their colour vision requirements are.

Engineer

You will be able to train as an engineer if you're colour blind, but many employers may reject you if you can't see colour properly. Engineers to a broad range of jobs that can involve many different things so some tasks will require good colour vision.

Once again, the guidelines aren't very clear so speak to some employers if you need more information.

Police officer

The blanket ban on colour blindness has been overturned but colour vision tests are still likely to be required. Rather than being rejected for failure of an

Ishihara test, candidates are considered on an individual basis and will be tested more thoroughly. Colour blind people do have a chance to become a police officer, but it is not certain.

Entering the police force may be possible for some colour blind people, but the condition will still affect some areas of work. For example, if another officer tells you that the suspect you are looking for is in a green top and you can't see green, further details will need to be given; which is time-consuming and impractical in a tense situation.

Armed forces

There is a colour blindness test to get into the military but as long as you pass all other tests it won't hold you back. There are some jobs within the armed forces that you'll be unable to do, such as piloting planes in the RAF, but most basic roles should hold no boundaries for you. However, some say that being colour blind is actually beneficial for a sniper as they don't see camouflage in the first place. The military is a very big organisation, so always research the requirements for your exact role if you want to specialise.

That ends the list of big careers impacted by colour blindness. Other less well known jobs may be affected by the condition; so if you're unsure speak to an employer. I will state the obvious in advising that jobs requiring the sole use of colour will be out of the question for colour blind people. These include decorators, designers, display makers and many more. Some professions may not require perfect colour vision, but it may be much harder without it; which could make the work less enjoyable.

CHAPTER 5 – ADVICE ON LIVING WITH COLOUR BLINDNESS

For the last four chapters I have merely been educating you on everything about colour blindness. For this one, I'll try to be helpful and give real life advice on how to deal with colour blindness. In this chapter, I'll offer some advice on how to deal with the condition, whether you've just been diagnosed and are a little taken-a-back or if you've known for years and just want some advice on how to go about your life.

Firstly, I will share my story about my diagnosis. I took the test as part of a routine eye check-up. I rarely went to the optician, but in previous visits I'd only had my actual eyesight tested. When I went for the test, I was shown some Ishihara plates and immediately failed. I got the blue-yellow plates but failed about 80% of the red-green plates.

When I left the optician, I was still surprised and had many questions racing through my head: *"How will this affect my future?" "Does this mean I won't be able to drive?" "Will I need extra help at school?"* I suppose I got a little worried and it hit me quite hard when I discovered that I'd never be able to pursue my dream job and become an airline pilot. It still saddens me to this day, but I guess you've just got to look past it.

I thought to myself: *"Right, time to rethink,"* I was racking my brain for alternatives that would not require perfect colour vision and none arose. Now in 6th form I still have no idea what I would like to do, apart from be self-employed; but that's ok. If you've discovered that your dream job is out of reach, don't let it bother you. If you're still at school, you've got plenty of time – it'll come to you eventually. If you've left school, don't panic! Find something else that you enjoy or that suits you well. There's no point in sitting there feeling sorry for yourself.

One thing that I find has helped me get to grips with my limitations has been writing this book. I guess being held back by my condition made me more passionate about spreading awareness and hopefully helping people discover what they can and can't do before it's too late. If you're feeling down about never reaching your dreams, do something else about it. Start a social media page or even a group at your school or workplace and chat to people who understand your problems and have similar issues. This can actually make you feel a lot better about the situation.

Pick a partner with good colour vision

If you've found someone with whom you would like to share your life, wouldn't it be helpful if they could be your colour adviser! Of course, if you've found the one and they share your condition, don't be pushed away because they won't be able to differ between colours for you. In fact, sharing the condition and sharing all of the funny flops that could occur as a result may well bring you closer together.

Refrain from colours that you can't see well

It may seem blatantly obvious, but for some they may not realise how useful it could be. For example, if you want a red Ferrari, but can't see red; you might end up with a green one. Of course, there'll be people to tell you which colours are green and red, but it isn't quite the same if it looks wrong to you. Perhaps, to avoid confusion, go for a black or white one, or simply one that is a colour that you can see well. It doesn't have to be boring. Not at all! Matte black is much more exciting than plain red!

Avoid the topic of colour if possible

Colour comes up in our lives all the time and we talk about it a lot as well. Of course, if you can't see it too well, you might feel a little left out. Not a problem! Just try to avoid the topic. So, for example, if you are at school and your friends are deciding whether to paint something red or green, or deciding which shade looks best; don't offer your advice! You could if you wanted to, I wouldn't force you not to. In fact, it could become a cracking prank or revenge. If someone who played a prank on you asks you to paint something green; paint it red – after all, you can't tell the difference. They might be quite annoyed, and you might feel rather smug *insert Jeremy Clarkson smug face here*.

If you've been asked to do a task that involves colour, politely decline. People should be fairly considerate and simply ask someone else who is colour able to do it. If they don't take note it's rude and disrespectful and you should report them to their seniors. Or you could just do a dreadful job of the task because you were unable to see properly and then make them look bad *insert evil laughing here*.

Ask for help if you're unsure about something that involves colours

This is another rather simple one, but it's a *very* useful tip. Of course, asking your friends and family to identify colours would be immediately obvious to you, but don't be afraid to ask people you don't know either. If you're embarrassed of your condition or don't like people knowing, don't be. People are generally very helpful and understanding. For example, I went into a shop to get some stationery and needed some highlighters. I couldn't tell which ones were green and yellow, and so asked one of the store assistants for help. They were more than happy to help and told me all that I needed to know. In short; don't be afraid to ask *anyone* for help, as they'll almost always be considerate and happy to help.

Use a system that doesn't require colour

We all have our various ways of sorting things out and keeping things in order in our lives, and many of us use colour. However, if you can't see colour very well, use another system. There are many out there; I'll mention some now, but there are plenty more out there to be found in the world of Google if you do a bit of digging.

Here are a few:

Use labels – although I may have mentioned it many times before, using labels is simple and very effective. Put simply, you can use labels for anything that's coloured. This could be pens, clothes, boxes or anything else that you can find. If you need to know the colour, write the name of the colour on that label. If you need to know the purpose/contents of the item, write that on the label.

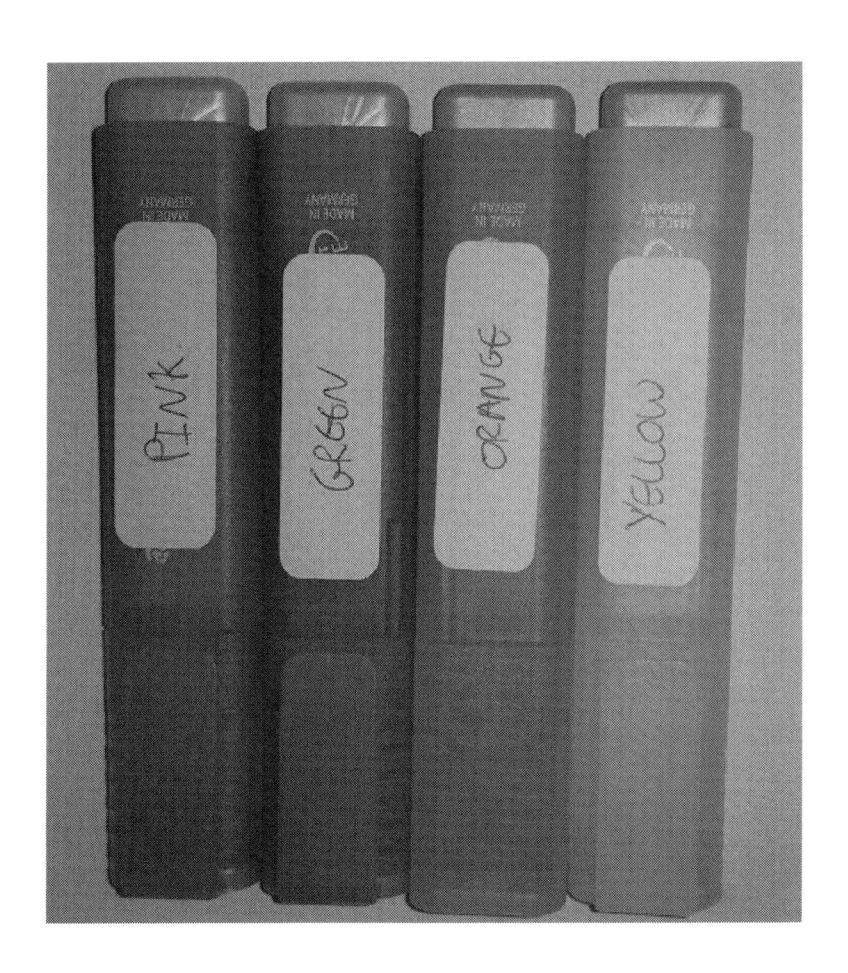

I labelled my own highlighters to make things easier. I can see a difference between them but I see the yellow one as light green. Though they are easier to see as pens, I find that it is harder to distinguish between the inks.

Use letters, numbers or shapes - some colour systems may be difficult to replace with labels or words. For example, take racing. Racing tracks will use mainly red, yellow and green flags to convey important messages. Red means stop, yellow means slow down and green means resume racing. Now, if you're travelling at high speed, you may not have time to read a word or phrase as you go past. However, you'll find it easy to interpret a letter, number or shape. I would think that using a circle to say stop, a triangle to say slow down and a square to say resume racing would work quite well. Perhaps I'll make a colour blind racing series one day.

We are all different and all have different needs, so if a system that would help you springs to mind, give it a go!

Don't splash out on things that improve colour - another weird one, but hear me out. I remember taking a trip to a TV shop and discovering the joys of OLED and QLED TVs. OLED TVs have an amazingly sharp picture and QLED ones have clear and bright colours. Now, TVs are not cheap, so if you're spending over a grand it's probably best to choose the right one. Obviously, if you can't see or tell the difference between colours too well, it doesn't make sense to buy something that should make colours appear brighter – you wouldn't notice the difference. The same would go for someone with good colour vision but blurred eyesight – they'd benefit from brighter colours. In short, don't bother with things that may improve things for others but not yourself.

Make your own database of colour - this one is a little complex to explain, but hopefully you'll understand. Though this will only really benefit those with anomalies, it's still a useful tip for all.

This one was triggered by something that occurred to me whilst walking along the street. I looked down at the side of the road and saw double "yellow" lines. I suddenly realised that in my eyes they were green, but all my life I'd been told they were yellow. My discovery linked to what the optician had told me when I was diagnosed; I had been told what colours things actually were by people all my life, so I shouldn't have too many problems with my condition.

This prompted me to think that I had subconsciously built up my own database of colour. Though most yellows in my eyes are green, I can sometimes tell if something is yellow by the shade of green that it is to me, if that makes sense. Going back to the double yellow lines, if something is the same shade of green in my eyes, then I can assume that it is actually yellow.

Chances are that many of you will have done this without actually knowing it. If you weren't diagnosed until you were older, you'll have probably been surrounded by colour able people in your early life, who'll have told you what colours things were; even if you couldn't see those colours properly.

If this isn't the case, it's not as hard as it sounds to start building up your own database. Just randomly ask your family or friends what colour something is and add it to your database. If something is actually yellow but you see it as a shade of green, make a mental note that it is yellow in real life. The next time you see a similar shade, you'll be more likely to know that it's actually yellow.

Admittedly, this will be harder if you've got full Protanopia, Deuteranopia or Tritanopia because you'll have no perception of certain colours at all and you'll be more likely to have known about your condition all your life; so people may not have told you the colour of things because they thought you wouldn't understand anyway. Still, worth a try.

Use time rather than colour - this tip will be most useful for the topic of food. Remember when I said that it can be harder to tell if a steak is cooked properly if you're colour blind? Well, that's where time can help. If you know that the perfect steak for you is cooked for 3 minutes on each side, time those 3 minutes rather than working out if it's cooked by eye. Do the same for other food, if you know that your cake will take 30 minutes to be perfectly brown on the top, put your faith in the clock rather than your own judgement.

This may not work in all instances, but it's worth a try and may be very effective.

Try glasses that correct colour blindness - I did some digging and managed to find some glasses that correct colour blindness. The way they work is that they spread wavelengths of colour out and essentially make colours appear brighter and clearer. Unfortunately, the technology is relatively new and is only affordably available to those with colour anomalies; as you need all three cones to see the whole spectrum. The cheapest ones that I found were about £40 but some more advanced ones from America cost up to $400! I will explain the benefits of these glasses in more depth in the next chapter.

CHAPTER 6 – MY EXPERIENCE WITH COLOUR BLIND GLASSES

For the purpose of this book and for my own research, I decided to try using a pair of colour blind glasses. We ordered them online for £79 and they were delivered within 2 days – smashing! We had to collect them from a small convenience store, meaning that we went out into town. I tried them on immediately and we went for to look around the town centre to see if I noticed any difference.

My first impression of the glasses was great. The ones we bought were Pilestone glasses they are rather nice. They have a tint which means they can also be a mirror in the right lighting from the outside, which is cool. They look like normal sunglasses; a simple yet sleek design that is also comfortable.

Here are the glasses. The tint looks different in different

lighting. In this case it is a brown-red tint. There are some un-tinted options but all will have a slight colour to them. I think they are smart!

This is the case. The glasses themselves are excellent

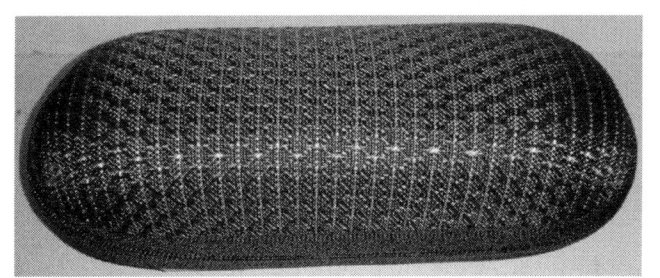

and look smart but they also come with this stylish case that is great quality. This includes a cleaning cloth.

We chose the medium-strong strength glasses. I would say that my colour blindness is medium-strong severity, so the weak-medium severity glasses would probably do the job almost as well. With any colour blind glasses there are usually either weak-medium or medium-strong strength and perhaps very strong options or some are separated according to the colour affected – green, red or blue.

The most popular and scientific brand seems to be Enchroma, a California-based firm that not only sells corrective glasses but also researches the impacts of colour blindness. We looked on the Enchroma website and were greeted by a whole host of information and a guide of all the products. The glasses they sell were mostly categorized as I mentioned before.

Enchroma also had a test available where you could essentially diagnose yourself with the type of your colour blindness and the severity. Though my glasses are not Enchroma ones, they work on basically the same principle, so I decided to take the test first with and without the glasses.

The test consisted of 20 or so Ishihara plates with answer options of numbers 1-9, unsure or nothing. Some of the questions mixed reds and greens, some greens and blues and some blues and reds. I was almost certain that I was deuteranomalous before taking the test but thought that it was medium strength. I found that I had the most trouble with the red-green patterns and the patterns where the shades of green differed. My results came back as *strong* deuteranomalous. I was surprised at how severe my condition was!

However, the second time round I used my glasses to see if they made a difference; and they did! During the second run, I would first look at the pattern without the glasses and then look at it with the glasses. I found that the glasses clearly separated reds, greens and browns for me where I couldn't distinguish in the first instance. Furthermore, they made it easier to determine if there was not a pattern in the first place – they separated shades of green very well.

There were still some patterns that I struggled with, but the number was greatly reduced with the glasses on and I found that I took less time deciding on each pattern – it seems that the glasses gave me more confidence in deciding which colours were which. The result of course was not perfect, but my *strong* deuteranomaly was reduced to *mild* deuteranomaly with the glasses on. A very positive result indeed!

Enchroma is a really great brand with a helpful website, but there is a single reason that I chose not to use Enchroma glasses – price. Their glasses start at around £200 and can go right up to £500. There is also a further shipping cost as they need to come all the way from California. However, I should mention that they have a range of indoor *and* outdoor glasses, as well as kids' ones; and that their glasses often include UV filter and therefore act as sunglasses as well. That kind of price is a little too steep for me now but if you feel like you want a pair of snazzy corrective glasses that double up as sunglasses, go for it!

As I said, when I first got the glasses, we went for a stroll around the town centre to see if I could notice any differences. I needed about 10-15 minutes to adjust to the glasses. At first, they were very similar to sunglasses. They made everything seem slightly darker. Even having adjusted to the now, they still darken the actual brightness of light that you see slightly.

However, once I got used to them, the brightness of the *colours* was much more intense. Even if colours were still unchanged, they appeared much brighter than they had done before. Sitting here writing this book, when I look out the window with the glasses off, the light is bright and white, but the trees are a greyish green. With the glasses on, the light is slightly darker, but the trees are a much brighter, fuller green.

In the shopping centre, I found that many shop signs that I had seen as certain colours all my life suddenly changed colour. For example, the *Boots* logo had always been a light bluish-purple, but it was a powerful, clear navy blue through the glasses. Then, there was a shop which had each letter of its name in different colours. Without the glasses, I saw two shades of green, orange and two shades of pink. With the glasses on, I saw orange, pink, *purple,* light green and for the first time every *yellow.* This was an interesting experience!

Being able to see different shades of colours clearly was quite amazing. We went into a clothes shop and I found a shirt that, in my eyes, looked like three shades of pink.

There was a darker shade and then two lighter ones which I really struggled to distinguish between. However, with the glasses on I could see that the darker shade was purple, the middle shade was red, and the lighter shade was pink. Furthermore, all these different shades stood out from each other very clearly.

Outside, though it was dark, I was still noticing differences. Traffic lights, to me, have always been orange, green, blue; as opposed to red, amber, green. With the glasses on, I was able to see red, orange and turquoise-green. Though this is not fully accurate, it is much closer to the actual colour than without glasses. Furthermore, my dad pointed out two green traffic lights where one was a slightly lighter colour. Without the glasses these shades were the same but with the glasses I was able to split the shades after looking at the lights for a moment or two.

Finally, on the way home we walked past a television on HiFi shop. Remember when I spoke a about OLED and QLED TVs? QLED TVs are the ones that deliver brighter colours. There was a QLED TV in the window and it had a clip for demonstration that included many bright and varied colours. Without the glasses, I was unable to appreciate the range, depth and brightness of the colours. With the glasses, I was able to see a wider range of colours *and* the colours appeared brighter. I now find that these glasses are particularly useful for computers and TVs.

It was very strange seeing true yellow properly for the first time. This has really shaken up my perception of colour and I feel like I will need many months to adjust to this new colour scheme. Previously, I mentioned that I have partly trained myself to co-ordinate real colours with shades of colours that I see. For example, double-yellow lines appear green to me, but I have trained my eyes to an extent to know that that shade of colour is yellow in real life.

Now that I have these glasses, this "training" process will have to start all over again. Now that I can see yellow, I will need to see all those previously green objects through the glasses and adjust them to yellow in my mind. The same goes for greens, reds and browns.

I do still find myself missing out yellow. I still see some shades of yellow that I was unable to see before as gold or orange, rather than green. For example, my yellow motorbike that was previously green I now see as gold through the glasses, even though it is metallic yellow. Still, this will all come with time.

One area that I am keen to test the glasses in is school, particularly geography. Geography is famous for colouring-in and even looking past the stereotype there is still a lot of colour involved. Colours are often used in pie charts, bar graphs, altitude maps, and choropleth maps. Choropleth maps can often use very small dots or squares of different shades of a certain colour, or different colours altogether. This is like an Ishihara test and is a real nightmare for a colour blind person.

My colour blindness has affected my work in geography before and my teacher asked if there was anything that could be done to help. These glasses should make things a lot easier and could make things much easier for other colour blind pupils all over the UK.

If you or someone you know is having trouble with colour blindness, I really recommend that you give the glasses a go. Though the Enchroma ones are very expensive and even my Pilestone ones are not cheap, there are some options out there that cost as little as £35. Give them a go as you really do notice an immediate difference and being able to see colours that you could not see before or tell the difference between shades that you would have merged before really will bring a smile to your face.

On a final note, these glasses could be the way to a better future for colour blind people. The research is relatively new, and it will be harder to correct dichromatic colour blindness with lenses, but I think that these glasses could be very useful in the future.

The majority of colour blind people are trichromatic and only have mild anomalies, meaning it could be very easy to correct deficiencies for most people with the condition. This would not only make the lives of most colour blind people easier but could also lead to them being able to pursue their dream career. For example, I could pursue my dream to become a pilot if I found some corrective lenses that had UV filters.

There is still a lot of research to be done and many industries will remain stringent on their entry requirements, even if you are able to amend your issue. However, there is hope and one day we could change the world for colour blind people.

That's it for the book! I hope that you learned something new or were maybe inspired to make a change. My final and most important message is this: don't let colour blindness limit you or drag you down. Instead, use it to innovate or inspire you to make your own dent in the universe. Rather than thinking about what you can't do, think about what you could change or how you could improve things. You never know, your colour blindness may lead to an idea that will make you the next multi-millionaire!

GLOSSARY

Congenital – present from birth.

Chromosome – structure of acids and proteins that carries genetic information in the form of genes.

Gene – unit of genetic information that hold various "codes" for different characteristics, found on chromosomes.

Dominant – gene that will have an effect even if paired with another gene. Will also "overpower" (stop the effects of) a faulty *recessive* gene.

Recessive – gene that is carried but needs another similar gene to have an effect; girls need two faulty genes to be colour blind as a single gene would be "overpowered" by a normal *dominant* gene.

Rods – receptive cells in the eye that are receptive to dim light.

Cones – receptive cells in the eye that are receptive to colour.

Anomaly – where someone has all their cones, but one is faulty or out-of-alignment. They will have some perception of all colours but will confuse different colour and shades.

Trichromacy – where someone has all three of their cones present.

Dichromacy – where someone has two of their cones present; one is completely missing. They will not be able to perceive the colour transmitted by the missing cone at all.

Monochromacy – where someone only has one cone present; the other two are completely missing. They will see life grey-scale.

Anomalous trichromat – someone who has all three of their cones present; but has one that is faulty or out-of-alignment.

Protanomaly – where someone has all three of their cones present, but has a faulty red cone meaning they will confuse red with other colours and mix shades of red.

Deuteranomaly – where someone has all three of their cones present, but has a faulty green cone meaning they will confuse green with other colours and mix shades of red. The majority of colour blind people are deuteranomalous.

Tritanomaly – where someone has all three of their cones present, but has a faulty blue cone meaning they will confuse blue with other colours, mainly yellow, and mix shades of blue. This is the rarest form of anomaly.

Protanopia – where someone has a red cone that is missing or completely dysfunctional. They cannot perceive red light and are dichromatic.

Deuteranopia – where someone has a green cone that is missing or completely dysfunctional. They cannot perceive green light and are dichromatic.

Tritanopia – where someone has a blue cone that is missing or completely dysfunction. They cannot perceive blue light and are dichromatic. This is a *very* rare form of colour blindness.

Cone monochromacy – where someone is two cones that are missing or completely dysfunctional. Only either red, green or blue light can be perceived but vision is often almost greyscale as the brain needs to compare different colours to be able to perceive colour.

Rod monochromacy (achromatopsia) – where someone is missing all three cones; no wavelengths of light are perceived, and vision is completely greyscale. People with this condition are often sensitive to bright light as rods respond to *dim* light. This is the rarest and most severe form of colour blindness.

Printed in Great Britain
by Amazon